LET THE WATER
RUN CLEAR

E. L. Dan

♡

Nicky, ♥
So great to meet you!!!...
xo Erin :)

LET THE WATER RUN CLEAR

poems by

E.L. Dan

Cover design by Tasha Ali
theunusualneedle.com
@unusualneedle

ISBN: 9798501232365

CONTENTS

WHERE THE HONEYSUCKLE GROWS

A LIGHT YOU CANNOT DIM

MEANT TO BE WILD

THE ACHE OF LIVING

REMEMBER THE LIGHT

For my six-year-old self.

WHERE THE HONEYSUCKLE GROWS

GROWING THROUGH THE MUD

Despite all of the doubt we carry, I know our bodies
are like harmonicas. I know there is music in our breath.

Somewhere, there are crickets asking us to dance.
Somewhere, there are flowers blooming in the dark.

Give me the lotus. Give me fistfuls of mud.
I want to know every inch of this world.

I want to hold the richness of it in my palms,
squeeze its juice between my fingertips, drink

it in until all of us are as full as the moon.
Do not give me a life painted only in one shade.

Give me a pitch-black sky until I am no longer
afraid of the dark. Let me chase after this life

and try to capture the fireflies knowing damn well
I cannot contain that kind of light.

Ask the butterflies about transformation—
they'll tell you of resilience, the ache, the doubt,

the pitch black unknowing, the sun swallowed into
the belly of the earth, the glistening promise of morning,

and then, the stretch, the freedom, the flight.
Meet me where the honeysuckle grows,

where we know, deep down in our bones,
that thorn and nectar, stretch and becoming,

are all part of the wild journey back home.

A STUDY OF FEAR AS AN ARTIST

press your hands to her sharpness.
trace her skull like a globe,
say: *this is where*
it all begins.
the place her madness turns to
magic. her mind, made of mud.
she plants trees in its belly.
she gathers up the ashes, kisses
their foreheads and they ask her:

do you promise that all of this pain
will be worth it?

do you promise to make it into
something beautiful?

ANGELS IN THE MARBLE

When Michelangelo was asked
how he sculpted David,

he said he simply chipped away
everything that was not him.

When I tell you that you are the artist,
that your words are your chisel,

and this world, in all of its brittle
heaviness, is your marble,

that your job is to answer your calling,
the one that keeps following you out into

the middle of that vast hallway,
what within you comes out of hiding?

What angels have always been there,
waiting, just below the surface?

A LETTER TO MY FEAR

When you knock
on the door I pretend
no one is home.

I watch you pace, like
a ghost, carrying yourself
like a car accident,

shrieking and then–
silence. A howl throws itself
off your lips and slides

under my door frame.
Fear, you have to believe me.
It is easier to turn off all the lights,

to close the blinds,
but I want to invite you to tea.
I want to sit with you on my sofa

and hold you while you cry.
Fear, there are days your shadow
is the only thing I can see.

If I am being honest,
I am terrified to lose you.
I don't know what my life

looks like without you.
I close my eyes and I am still the
same six-year-old girl terrified

of thunderstorms,
who is desperate for her mother
to tell her it will be okay and mean it,

for her father to stop sprinting
in the other direction of you,
who is convinced this world isn't

big enough to hold all of her shine.
Fear, for most of my life my body
was a hand-me-down I could never fit into,

but I am here now, and I refuse to ignore you.
I am so tired of running. Please, come in.
Sit down. I am listening.

FINAL OFFERING

i was six years old when the tree
in my backyard was struck by lightning.
i didn't see it happen, but i imagine
that it held its limbs like a final offering
to the sky—its flowers—ten thousand
white flags. my father cut down its charred
limbs the summer before he and my mother
got divorced. it was the fourth of july
and my sister was inside talking on the telephone.
the cord stretched like an arm through
the kitchen to the steps where she was sitting.
i don't remember where my mother and i
were in the house, i just know that when
my father nearly cut off his finger with the chainsaw,
he didn't say anything. instead, he walked calmly to
the kitchen, ran his hand under the faucet and
spilled into the sink. i can still see the blood—
how stark and stunning it was against the
stainless steel. how it poured in an endless
procession down the drain. tell me,
is this what it means to be a man?
to carry your softness to the water and
drown it in secret? to think that if anyone
were to see you spilling like this,
things would never be the same?

THE WAY IT HAS TO BE

When we push away our pain—
when we tell ourselves this is the
way it has to be—

when we say:
not now
not again
you are too much
a burden
a bother
a chore.

I imagine it swims to the
deep end of the lake,
holds its breath
under the surface
in protest,

counts to one thousand
and thinks we will
return to save it,
but we don't.

We are silent,
frozen.

When we
don't return,
it grows gills—
forgets what
the sun
looks like—
tells itself
this is the way
it has to be.

17

PATHWAYS

when my mind narrows
its pathways,
when it spirals
like a staircase
in a haunted house,

when all i smell is mold,
when the plump walls
threaten to release
a river of grief,
i trace the mantle

with my fingers,
check for dust
above the fireplace,
i am here so often
nothing has the chance

to settle,
i am a child convinced
they will always be the
same age.
i keep returning

to this place too small
for me to fit in.
*what is mine and
what isn't?*
i am convinced

there is no way out,
even though my
fists remember
breaking the glass—

the moment
each window
becomes a time machine
and i remember what
i had forgotten:
this is all temporary.

the sun will always
come back for me.

YOUR TRUE NATURE

You are being called back home
to yourself,

called back to the place
within you where the
porchlight never goes out,

even during the storm.
The one the moths swarm to,

where they brave the possibility
of annihilation for the chance
to become the light.

Let everything within you
that is not love turn to ash.

Tend to the kindling.
Stoke the flame.
Go where the rivers meet

themselves again.
You turn over a new leaf

every time you refuse to deny
your true nature.
Your true nature is love.

Let this swallow you whole.

A LIGHT YOU CANNOT DIM

RINSE AND REPEAT

you do not have to marry a good, christian
boy. the kind of man you know your mother
would love. you do not have to tether yourself
to her idea of safety. it is not your job to make
everyone comfortable. you were not made for
small love. you are the ocean. do not soak
yourself in apology or splinter your hands with
the wreckage. you are not selfish for taking care
of yourself. you do not have to be the lifeboat
or the sunrise. you are the steam rising from
water. you are the fog, finally clearing. release
this poison shame you are wearing like
perfume. smash all the bottles. pray for rain.

INTUITION
after Sierra DeMulder

My truth chews on my ears,

    glides itself up my skin,

licks the salt off the back of my neck,

    inches its way in between

my eyebrows, sits, perched,

    a glowing radiant worm,

waiting to be noticed. My third eye

    keeps it safe, my intuition

surfaces after the rain—wet on the sidewalk,

    crawling towards the mud,

where the truth becomes and

    unbecomes itself.

It waits for me to open—to realize

    nothing truly exists except

the movement of it all: the breath,

    the body, the spirits soaring—

becoming and unbecoming themselves.

LET ME GO

What a noble martyr, sacrificing
your own happiness.

What a thankless journey, a lonely
swim to nothing.

Their acceptance is what keeps you
from suffocating.

They tell you *you are beautiful*
and the color floods your cheeks.

They tell you *you are helpful*
and your gills open like a geyser.

If you could, what would you ask
of the fisherman?

WHAT IF LOVING ME

is like trying to drink water
out of two cupped
palms?

what if you are always
thirsty?

THE MORNING AFTER THE STORM

the air is an empty lung.

I pick up all of the garbage with my hands:
the glass bottles, a gutted bag of chips.

The wind is heavy with apology:
I'm so sorry, I don't know what got into me.

The tantrums that destroy
entire cities:

I'm sorry, I can fix it.
Look at that bright sun,

her promise to wipe the memory
clean. If you close your eyes

it's almost like nothing
ever happened.

HOW TO COME OUT
after Andrea Gibson

Release the termites. Let them chew a gap
in the closet door. Teach them to be naked
and persistent. Do not attach a single explanation
to their backs. You do not owe anyone an apology.

I know some say that we are an abomination—years of
fingerprints pressing their rights and wrongs into the
malleable clay of our hearts, of our gender, of our sex.
Do not forget: the body and god are not separate.

Do not forget. Forgive them for their one-sided minds,
their hate speech, then let them go. Free them from curling
up into your tendons and tying knots between your
shoulder blades. Let the heaviness go. It only holds you
back and you,

you are a creature of movement. Say: *This is my body.*
When they ask you to identify with habitual labels,
box you in until the suffocation of stagnant air tries to
strangle your ballooning lungs, tell them.

Tell them how the trees change in the spring.
Ask them for their baby pictures. Be the boomerang,
the shoreline, the moon. Whatever you do,
forget what it feels like to stay one place.
Shake the iron from your legs.
Walk through that door again
and again and again saying:

Here I am. I am made of a light you cannot dim.
I am a ship who will not abandon its harbor.
I do not know who I will be tomorrow,
in four hours, or even this evening,

but I am still going to be here praising my body
for loving what it loves.

Love what you love.
Leave the rest to puddle at their feet.
Promise me you'll keep walking and
when you're ready
ask them:

Will you walk with me?

MEANT TO
BE WILD

ON BECOMING

you do not have to be pretty. you do not have to rinse clean the feeling of too much wine and not enough toothpaste. you do not have to put away the laundry, or wash the towels, or clean the mud off the hardwood. you only have to breathe. settle into your stacked spine. you do not have to be balance or support beam. you do not have to know where the light is to know you deserve it.

meanwhile, the cat is curled up under the window. meanwhile, the dog twitches in his sleep, and you are worried about having enough money, enough time. you read books on how to *become*.

meanwhile, you already are.

WORST THING

"I am not the worst thing I've said about myself"
    after Tonya Ingram

I am not the shame, or the anxiety, or the hum of loneliness
that steals the joy from my chest. I am not the fear that
sweeps this house clean, the unworthiness that flosses its
teeth with me. I am not the anger or the ache of nightfall.

I am not the depression, the panic, or the pain.
I am not my history, not the sting or the hopelessness,
not the dread or the silence. I am not what lives inside me
that wishes I would stop telling stories.

I am not what tries to protect my shame.
I am not what tells me I am unlovable,
selfish, a burden too big for anyone to bear,
a record too broken to play.

I am the song—honest, raw,
vibrating up to the balcony of my throat—
rushing to welcome home that first sacred note,
arms wide open, echoing back to you.

QUICK AS I CAN

When I am running, quick as I can,
away from myself,

when I am looking for someone to blame
for the drought,

my body is always the first I point to—
the wild animal I try to stuff into a cage.

The one I scoff at and say:
if you were only smaller,

if your stomach was less balloon
and more windowpane,

if your thighs were more branch
than tree trunk,

if the skin of your arms did not hang
like rotten fruit—

then you would be happy.

SIT/STAY/WAIT

There are days I treat my
stomach like a disobedient

circus animal. I ask her to sit,
stay, wait,

to walk on her hind legs,
but she refuses.

She is a bear I try
to stuff into a tutu—

a lion tired of jumping
through hoops.

I tell her she'll never be ready
for the stage. I hide her behind

the curtains, curse her name,
cart her around but never let her

see the crowd.
I am ashamed to admit

how I've wished she would
disappear altogether,

how I've wished she was a koi fish
swimming in circles beneath

the flat, frozen,
surface of the lake.

What a curse this is,

to wish your body was the

opposite of your feelings:
small, gentle, obedient.

There is nothing beautiful
about taming something

meant to be wild.

LET THEM BE

their bodies,
just like ours,
are not anyone's
to use.

A STUDY OF SUFFERING AS A DAIRY COW

Her worth is defined by her body's ability to give.
She is corralled into a fluorescent warehouse
for a third time today, hooked up to the cold metal
that lessens the swelling but never the pain.

She closes her eyes and pretends
she is feeding her baby.

The cement below her becomes
a meadow where all of the blades lift
to kiss the bottoms of her hooves.

She closes her eyes and imagines her child
beside her, dozing off under the warmth
of the sun, chewing cud in a field of poppies.

Here, there is no mention of her body—
no mention of the ballooning tapeworm
between her legs—here, it has burst into a
kaleidoscope of butterflies.

Here, it is no longer a swollen
heartbeat, a poison apple,
a death sentence.

She opens her eyes
and all she sees is gray.

She opens her eyes and remembers
the hands that will keep taking and taking
what is not theirs, until she is empty,

until her body is a still,
lifeless machine.

MIRACLE BODY

I'm sorry I compare you to bruised fruit.

I'm sorry I come crawling back to you
immediately after cursing your existence.

I'm sorry I don't acknowledge that you are
the one who rebuilds the wreckage.

I'm sorry I put up the caution tape when I think
you are too much a crime scene for anyone else to see.

I'm sorry I search for approval in the mouths
of strangers. I'm sorry I've made homes in bodies

that were not you. I'm sorry for worshipping
the deity of my suffering, for bowing at their feet,

even though it means you as the sacrifice.
I'm sorry for the shame I hold hostage under your skin.

I'm sorry for telling you that you are anything but a miracle
of a body–swing set of a person, bungee jumper,

you are the queen of bouncing back.
You have been with me every step of the way.

I'm sorry for not praising every inch of your terrain,
for not telling you every day that you are proof of

resilience, that flowers bloom every time I'm brave enough
to speak your truth.

I am living on holy ground. I am alive because you refuse to
give up on me.

THE VOICE THAT GUIDES YOU

let your heart be the voice that guides you / the one you turn to when you're hooked on a thought / remember the tale of the koi fish who swam all the way to the top of the waterfall / how the gods turned them into a golden dragon to honor their perseverance / you do not have to fear your own power / fall back in love with your breath / with being right where your feet are planted / notice how your body does not question, and question, and question everything / but receives / witnesses / notice how much you are resisting your own rhythm / trust this drumbeat even when your mind tells you not to / remember, your thoughts are not facts / some days you will think and think and think yourself into submission / these thoughts are meant to be witnessed, not caught / let your light fill the blue sky / swim all the way to that golden horizon line / watch as your gills turn to lungs / laugh when they tell you you cannot / be your own hero / prove them wrong.

LETTER TO MYSELF, AGE 16

One day, you will no longer be afraid
of your thoughts.

Your eating disorder will no longer be yours
to carry. It will be a distant memory,

the abusive relationship you left once
you could see clearly.

You will not wake every morning basing
your worth off of how flat your stomach is.

Each night will not be spent calculating exactly
how much "guilt" you digested that day.

Your feelings will no longer be something
you run from.

One day, you will be alone in your college
apartment and expect it to show up,

to taunt you with your own solitude the way it did
every day for four years but it doesn't.

It is the skeleton you freed from the closet,
the scale you finally decided to throw away.

One day, you will actually believe that food is fuel.
You will start to enjoy cooking again,

just like when you were little. You will find so many
similarities between you and your younger self.

Trust her, she is the key to your authenticity.
She lived a life before the shame set in.

One day, you will enjoy exercising again.
You will stop when your body wants to stop

and once, on a run,
you will catch yourself saying:

I love you
I love you
I love you

over and over like a tribute to your heartbeat,
like a song you've known the words to all this time.

The enemy has never been your body.
Your body wants nothing more than to support you.

It is both the sunrise and the horizon line. It has been
aching to be on your team.

Your brain is doing the best it can with the chemicals
it is given. It is not weak to ask for help.

In fact, it is the strongest thing you ever will do.
You will learn how to let others support you.

You will learn to speak your truth even when it's not easy.
And no, it won't always be easy.

There will be days, entire weeks, when your body feels like
both the weapon and the victim.

When you drool over the thought of breaking open,
when there is a chorus of "too much" beating against

your skin. But remember: your body is your shelter.
Even if the whole world is up in flames,

you are made of ocean.
Do not destroy your only life vest.

This is where your power lives.
This is the song redemption sings.

This is what healing looks like,
not a pretty picture, but a frame

carved with your name.
Come home to yourself.

Come home to yourself.
Come home.

I promise,
it will all be worth it.

THE ACHE
OF LIVING

WRITING THE POEM

Instead of writing the poem, I mash an avocado.
I toast bread, grind the pink crystals from the glass jar.

I pluck my eyebrows. I put on foundation. I burn incense,
open all the windows. I hold a Turquoise stone to my
throat.

I pick a Tarot card, pray inspiration strikes me like Cupid's
arrow, lifts me up to meet my Highest Self.

My sister asks how it's going and I tell her my words are
garbage–a sea of dead batteries and plastic bottles, a
mountain of Styrofoam.

Instead of writing the poem, I cry. Instead of writing the
poem, I get angry. I breathe. I rest into this moment and
I let it hold me.

Today, this is the only thing I know how to do.

THE LIFE OF MY FEELINGS

My disappointment wanders outside
mid-afternoon, makes their way to the
garden where they pick all of the produce
before it is ripe, comes inside to sulk
in the tub, meets my sadness for lunch
where both of them eat, silent, except
for the scraping of their plates.

My rage frequents two places: the gym,
where they use their fists to expel the desire
to turn everything to ash, and the Internet,
where they scroll their way to nightmare,
and wake, soaked in sweat.

My self-doubt prefers jogging or bird watching,
enjoys gazing at the cageless glory of each
winged creature—often catches themselves
speaking out into the crisp autumn air to no one
in particular: *I wonder how long it will take them to
realize they can go anywhere. I wonder how long it will be
until they realize they are free.*

PRETTY LITTLE BEAST

"That pretty little beast, a poem,
has a mind of its own."
        -Mary Oliver

Some days, I ask them to be intimidating
and instead, they roll over onto their back
to show me their belly.

Some days, I want them to play fair and
instead, they go right for the jugular.

Some days, I ask them to write about the
the sun, the stars, the moon but instead,
they refuse to focus on anything other than

the year that changed both of us forever,
keep circling back to the same fruitless city.

You're safe now, I tell them, *you don't have to
keep walking down the alley we both know
leads to nothing. We did the best we could.*

Even now, as they pretend to sit quietly
in the corner, I can see their wheels turning:

*There must be something we could have done
differently. There must be some way to rewrite
the ending.*

WORM MOON

As the ground softens,
as the air kisses our cheeks
and welcomes us into a new
season, remember that being
gentle with yourself is, in itself,
an act of rebellion.

Face the mirror of the sky and
see yourself for the first time:
a full, radiant, force of nature.

Watch the stars as they stand
hand in hand, listen as they ask us
to melt together like the tail of a comet,
to soften beneath their feet,
to remember that we are all made
of the same dirt.

FOR COREY

I am riding on the back of your motorcycle.
We are going 65 under a clear, July sky.
Everything is sun-soaked and golden.
I close my eyes as the hum of the wind cocoons me.

We are two bluebirds flying just to remind
themselves they are free.

Here, there is no pain.
We are not the ache or the urge to numb it.
We are not the past or the threat of it repeating.
We are not the future–the heartbreak, the wreckage,
the words we threw like daggers into the soft plywood
of each other's chests.

Here, everything is quiet and tender.
Here, we vow to drink in this moment
before it passes through the cups of our hands.

Do you remember the time we swam in that freezing
pool at the bottom of the waterfall in Hector?

How hard we laughed when you dropped that crowler of
beer trying to swim to the other side?

I can still remember how it felt to be let into the vault of
your heart–the golden light that escaped when you felt safe
enough to drop the walls.

Somewhere, you are a winged creature flying high
in a sun-soaked sky.

Somewhere, you are riding motorcycles, painting
masterpieces, playing the banjo and singing

with your whole body. You are everything
you've always wanted to be.

You are free.

WITH THESE WORDS

The reason I am alive is not to push
away the fear, pain, grief, or anger
but to invite them in and say:

I see you. I know you are temporary,
fleeting. You are not who I truly am.
Thank you for being here. What are
you trying to tell me?

With these words I take back
my power.

I set down my sword,
knowing my feelings
are just another part of me
that want to be loved, held,
understood, and then,

like a cloud of bats,
or a murder of crows,
be set free into the night sky–

emptied from my body like an exhale.
Here I stand, anchored in this ocean body.

This is all part of the holy dance.
This is what it means to take back
your power, your tenderness, your grit,

to not resist the most human parts
of us but to love them all–

to love them so much
they let you go.

COLLAPSING

When everything
around you is on fire,

when the swell
of the pain can
no longer hold you,

when the lightning
strikes and the sky
turns crimson,

remember that you
have the ability to turn
your body into a river,

to refuse to spark
anything that does not
lead others to safety,

to hold space for those
still making their way out
of the fog,

still wondering if there is
life after the storm.

Even when you feel
like you have none
of the answers,

remember that they
have always been
written in your chest,

in your ability to share
your story, to show
your scars and say:

yes, I almost turned to ash
trying to be what I know now
I was never destined to be.

I know now I am
this entire city.

I am not separate
from the birds,
or the telephone wire,

the fire escapes,
or the hum of the subway
just beneath our feet.

Your story is your superpower.

It is what rescues others from
the burning buildings inside
of our heads.

Go, do not wait till
you are ready.

YEAR AHEAD

What within you will
take flight this year?

What winged creature
will emerge from your
body like a phoenix?

What hope lies beneath
your doubt like a panting
animal?

What solace has always
been yours to lean into?

What is waiting to fill you
with what you were sure
went down with the ship

but here it is,
standing before you in all of
its stunning audacity:

the wonder, the warmth,
the possibility that there is more

to this life than just the ache of
living.

REMEMBER
THE LIGHT

ANATOMY OF A LIGHTHOUSE

We are made of
tissue and tendon,

skin and sweat.
Our lungs swell

and stretch
to return us

to this moment's
doorstep.

Your heart,
as heavy as

it may seem,
is a buoy

humming
itself to sleep

on the slick, black
surface of the ocean.

Your heart,
made of salt

and water,
seaweed and sand,

is not separate
from any of it.

The universe wants

nothing more than to

help us brave the storm,
to carry our hearts

back to shore
and ask the stars

again under the
slick, black sky:

This is the reason
for all of the darkness

isn't it?

To remind me of
the lighthouse

inside of my chest?

Yes.
Yes.
Yes.

FINGERPRINTS

I tell you I don't like writing love poems
because they are cliché, but the truth is,
I don't like doing things I'm not very good at,
and I am only just starting to be really good
at loving you.

I'm still fairly new at being honest about my
feelings and not letting my own truth rot in
my mouth.

The truth is, it's much easier for me to write
about the darkness and how I found my way out
than it is to describe how it makes me feel when
we slow dance in the kitchen, when you smile
at me in your sleep, or how beautiful you are
when you read.

The truth is, I've spent so many days writing
about the ways I've come home to myself
and haven't written any about what it feels like
to come home to you.

The truth is, I don't want you to look for your
fingerprints in my poems and not find a trace of you.

You, who made me believe in love again.
You, who I want to do real life with.
You, who somehow wants to do life with me,

even when I'm mean and grumpy at the grocery store.
Even when I tell you you're screaming even though
you're talking at a normal volume,
but I get overstimulated easily.

Even when I'm talking about gender and pronouns
and the patriarchy and the conversation ends and then
you start telling me about what kind of wood grain
you prefer for our next home and which ones you dislike
and I somehow take it as a metaphor for gender and think
you're judging me.

I imagine being with me is like being in love with a cotton
candy machine, or a tornado, or a tumbleweed.

I imagine you have to be really good at staying on your feet.

The truth is, I've never met anyone I want to do
life with more than you, never appreciated anyone
else's sweet tooth, and I want you to know,

deep down in your roots, that all of my poems
have your name written in them,
even when they don't.

You are part of my best parts, my honest parts,
my mundane, my joyous, my hopeful,

you are part of it all.

SO OFTEN

your mind runs ahead so often / your body forgets what day it is / sink your teeth into this moment / let the juice drip down your chin / call your gratitude back / let whatever must be done wait until tomorrow / the sunset needs you to see it off / the bats are calling your name out into the crisp autumn air / you hold your heart to the sky against the backdrop of purples and blues / the world dims to night / you walk home to yourself / you are even more you than you were yesterday.

TODAY I THOUGHT TO MYSELF

I just want to write something honest, something brave,
something about how I am still afraid of being seen
beneath my poems–the human me–the one with hands and
feet and a vat of self-doubt I try to decorate with fancy,
embroidered pillows and coffee-stained upholstery.

I worry that if I show people who I really am, behind all of
the rhythm and gloss of words, it will feel like going to a
movie you are so excited to see only to realize the trailer
was better.

It's not that I'm trying to make you feel exhilarated all of
the time–although, I do want to remind you of the lush
green garden within you, the one where all of the answers
you've been seeking sit, sipping tea in big hats in the
afternoon sun, waiting patiently for you to notice them,
laughing at your idea of perfection–

I just don't want you to miss the mundane. The mornings
you stand in the kitchen making coffee, your mind running
ahead to all of the things *you must you must you must* get done,
so much so that you miss the way the coffee grounds
scatter across the countertop like a galaxy of stars, the way
the first sip lingers on your tongue.

This morning, I was listening to a meditation teacher who
said they want to remind us that we don't have to devote all
of our time to trying to heal ourselves. That we aren't some
project to be fixed, some unruly garden that will *one day one
day one day* be good enough, that we deserve to drink in the
fullness of this honest, beautiful life.

All of it, already enough, just as it is.

SACRED HEART

There will be months you search for your own, kind, heart
in the reflection of the water but instead are greeted by a
carnival of doubt–the surface clouded by mud and debris–
creatures who will not stop circling with their sharp tails
and tongues and you convince yourself this is how it will
always be.

And then, there will be a morning–one where you are just
beginning to unzipper yourself from the night–when you
do not expect to find yourself again, but you do, find
yourself again, softer now. This whole time you've been
here. You never left.

Stay for the times you remember and the times you forget.
Your sacred heart loves them both.

WHAT I'VE LEARNED ABOUT FEELING

1. Holding on to resentment is like drinking poison and expecting the other person to die. However, anger is necessary. Anger is what keeps me alive the times I refuse to stand up for myself. It is the voice inside of me saying: *you deserve so much better than this. You deserve so much better. Get up, girl. You are your own worst enemy.*

2. There are a thousand ways we harm ourselves–none of them will ever be as dangerous as letting shame win.

3. Everyone is trying the best they can with the knowledge, understanding, and awareness they have. We are all searching for the warmth. The warmth can be a product of the liquor, the cigarettes, the hunger, the closeness, the breath. Anything to remind us we are alive. We are all a swirl of blood and tendon and need.

4. Recovery is not a linear process. It is way more roller coaster than straight line but taking four steps forward and three steps back still means you are moving ahead. You are growing so much every second, even when you can't see it.

5. When you want to give up, remember the first time your skin met the sunlight, the feeling of standing by the ocean or under the night sky, when you knew there was something bigger than this aching body, something bigger than this hurt. Remember how content you were as a baby–how you never questioned being hungry, sad, scared or lonely. The times you allowed your feelings the space to surface and dissipate as they do, even now. Do you remember?

6. There is a Buddhist meditation where you pretend you are seeing everything for the very first time. Every running faucet, every light turned on, is a magic trick. There is a magic trick inside of your chest. Your heartbeat, your muscles, they are all rooting for you.

7. The day you were born the sun was so excited to meet you. They were as proud as parent, giddy as spring, voice blooming: *Look what I made: the most perfect seed.*
I can't wait to see all the ways in which they will grow.

Wherever you go, remember the light. It is always there even when you don't see it. Even when you feel like you don't deserve it, it will always be rooting for you.

ACKNOWLEDGEMENTS

Thank you to my mom, my sister, my dad, my Baka, my Tete, and all of my family and friends who have always believed in me and my writing. Your support means more to me than I can even express. I would also like to extend my most sincere gratitude to everyone who donated to my Indiegogo campaign to help make this book possible.

A special thank you to Margaret, John, and Brisa for helping me with this process, and Tasha for creating such a beautiful cover for the book.

And to Sam—thank you for being my biggest fan and for always being there encouraging me to shine brightly, even on my darkest days. I'm so endlessly in awe of and grateful for you and our life together.

Thank you all for journeying alongside me. I love you.

ABOUT THE AUTHOR

Erin Dansevicus, E.L.Dan, is an artist, poet, reiki practitioner, activist, and owner of her own small business, Rooted In Courage, which utilizes the healing modalities of poetry, reiki, and meditation in order to hold space for and empower others. While this is their debut book, Erin's writing goes back a decade. Beginning her writing journey as a teenager in recovery from an eating disorder, Erin continues to find healing through writing and hopes to inspire others to share their story and connect with their authentic voice. She currently resides in Athens, GA with her girlfriend and their rambunctious dog. You can connect with her at @rootedincourage on Instagram or at rootedincourage.com.

Made in the USA
Middletown, DE
11 June 2023